D0759202

THE STORY OF THE
PHILADELPHIA 76ERS

THE NBA:
A HISTORY
OF HOOPS

THE STORY OF THE
PHILADELPHIA 76ERS

JIM WHITING

CREATIVE EDUCATION

Published by Creative Education
P.O. Box 227, Mankato, Minnesota 56002
Creative Education is an imprint of The Creative Company
www.thecreativecompany.us

Design and production by Blue Design
Art direction by Rita Marshall
Printed in the United States of America

Photographs by Corbis (Bettmann, Steve Lipofsky),
Getty Images (Andrew D. Bernstein/NBAE, Kim Blaxland,
Nathaniel S. Butler/NBAE, Focus on Sport, Jesse D.
Garrabrant/NBAE, Barry Gossage/NBAE, Drew Hallowell,
Walter Iooss Jr./NBAE, Neil Leifer/NBAE, Fernando
Medina/NBAE, Manny Millan/Sports Illustrated, Peter
Read Miller/Sports Illustrated, Photo Library/NBAE, Dick
Raphael/NBAE, Dick Raphael/Sports Illustrated, Jon
SooHoo/NBAE, John G. Zimmerman/Time Life Pictures),
Newscom (EMMANUEL DUNAND/AFP/Getty Images,
Chris Szagola/Cal Sport Media, Chris Szagola/ZUMA
Press)

Library of Congress Cataloging-in-Publication Data
Whiting, Jim.
The story of the Philadelphia 76ers / Jim Whiting.
p. cm. — (The NBA: a history of hoops)
Includes index.
Summary: An informative narration of the Philadelphia
76ers professional basketball team's history from its 1946
founding as the Syracuse Nationals to today, spotlighting
memorable players and events.
ISBN 978-1-60818-444-6
1. Philadelphia 76ers (Basketball team)—History—Juvenile
literature. I. Title.

GV885.52.P45W45 2014
796.323'640974811—dc23   2013039312

CCSS: RI.5.1, 2, 3, 8; RH.6-8.4, 5, 7

First Edition
9 8 7 6 5 4 3 2 1

Cover: Forward Thaddeus Young
Page 2: Center Dewayne Dedmon
Pages 4–5: Guard Hal Greer (#15), center Wilt
Chamberlain (#13)
Page 6: Forward/guard Andre Iguodala

TABLE OF CONTENTS

FROM SYRACUSE TO PHILADELPHIA 8

DR. J CURES THE 76ERS' AILMENTS 18

PHILADELPHIA FEELING 24

IVERSON IS "THE ANSWER" 30

UP AND DOWN … AND UP AGAIN? 34

INDEX 48

COURTSIDE STORIES

THE SHOT CLOCK BEGINS TICKING 11

HITTING THE CENTURY MARK 16

A PATRIOTIC NAME 20

CHAMPIONSHIP CITY 27

LISTENING TO THE ZINK 39

ADDING BY SUBTRACTING 44

INTRODUCING…

DOLPH SCHAYES 12

HAL GREER 15

JULIUS ERVING 23

MAURICE CHEEKS 29

CHARLES BARKLEY 37

ALLEN IVERSON 43

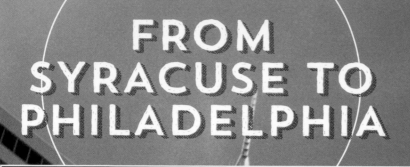

FROM SYRACUSE TO PHILADELPHIA

**W**ith the exception of Boston, Massachusetts, no American city is more closely associated with the establishment of the United States than Philadelphia, whose name means "City of Brotherly Love." The Declaration of Independence was signed there on July 4, 1776. The city hosted the convention that drafted the U.S. Constitution. Philadelphia was the home of Benjamin Franklin and other Founding Fathers. Millions of visitors flock to the city to see revolutionary-era landmarks such as Independence Hall, Congress Hall, and the Liberty Bell.

Not all the city's landmarks are connected to that era. Fairmount Park, the largest landscaped urban park in the U.S., is home to the country's oldest zoo. The house where Edgar Allan Poe wrote some of his most famous

ALEX HANNUM BECAME THE FIRST COACH TO WIN CHAMPIONSHIPS WITH TWO NBA TEAMS.

works attracts many visitors. There are more outdoor statues and other forms of public art in Philadelphia than in almost any other city in the world. And perhaps most recognizable of all are the steps leading up to the Philadelphia Museum of Art, which actor Sylvester Stallone made famous in the 1976 film *Rocky*. A bronze statue of Rocky stands nearby. The steps and statue reveal another side of Philadelphia that is perhaps as obvious as its historical importance. It is a city with a passion for sports. Philadelphia is one of just four American cities to have franchises in all four major professional sports located within its city limits: football's

Eagles, baseball's Phillies, hockey's Flyers, and basketball's 76ers.

The history of pro basketball in Philadelphia began with the Warriors, formed in 1946 as an original member of the Basketball Association of America (BAA). The Warriors won the league's first championship, and when the BAA merged with the rival National Basketball League (NBL) in 1949 to form the National Basketball Association (NBA), Philadelphia continued its winning ways. In 1956, the Warriors captured the NBA championship.

But in 1962, the team and its star player—center and Philadelphia native Wilt

JRUE HOLIDAY

THE SHOT CLOCK BEGINS TICKING

In the NBA's early days, fans disliked the slow pace. As *Sports Illustrated* writer Leigh Montville explains, "The strategy of the day had become inaction. Get a lead. Hold the ball. Go to the foul line. Make the foul shots. Teams were deciding to stall earlier and earlier in the game." Fans stayed away in droves, threatening the league's very existence. Syracuse Nationals owner Danny Biasone believed that forcing teams to take more shots would generate the excitement that would fill the seats. "Teams were taking about 60 shots in a game if nobody screwed around," he said. He wanted to double that number. So he divided 2,880 seconds (the length of a game) by 120 to get 24. The 24-second shot clock was instituted at the start of the 1954–55 season, and average combined scores increased by more than 14 points a game that season. While the game has undergone many other rule changes, the shot clock has remained at 24 seconds. "It's one of those intrinsically perfect, wonderfully illogical, perfectly imperfect numbers, like 9 innings in baseball and 18 holes in golf," says former NBA guard Mike Newlin. "It's an orphan number that fits perfectly into the family of basketball."

DOLPH SCHAYES

POSITION FORWARD / CENTER
HEIGHT 6-FOOT-7
NATIONALS / 76ERS SEASONS
AS PLAYER 1949–64
AS COACH 1963–66

Dolph Schayes played as a 76er for only one season. By the time the Syracuse Nationals moved to Philadelphia in 1963, Schayes had already logged 14 seasons with the team and was widely regarded as one of its biggest stars. But he had never expected to enjoy such steady success. He signed a one-year contract in 1949. "That one year," he said, "turned into 16 years." Schayes was an old-school player, relying on a two-handed set shot to score the bulk of his 18,438 career points, even after the one-handed jump shot had become the most popular way to score. He was equally aggressive on offense and defense and a sure shot at the free-throw line—qualities that helped as player/coach during the team's first season in Philadelphia. After playing 24 games in 1963–64, Schayes retired as a player but stayed on as coach for 2 more seasons. His son Danny also played in the NBA, retiring in 1999 after an 18-year career during which he scored 8,780 points—less than half the total his dad put up.

FORWARD CHET "THE JET" WALKER USED HARD DRIVES TO THE HOOP TO DRAW FOULS.

> ## "WE HAVE A SOLID CORE OF ABOUT 1,000 LOYAL FANS. NEXT YEAR, THIS SHOULD INCREASE TO ABOUT 2,500 FOR EVERY GAME."
> — OWNER IKE RICHMAN ON EARLY SUPPORT FOR THE TEAM

Chamberlain—moved west to San Francisco. Pennsylvania's diehard hoops fans were devastated. In the spring of 1963, a pair of local businessmen bought the NBA's Syracuse Nationals and brought that team to Philadelphia.

The Nationals had joined the NBL in 1946, when bowling alley owner Danny Biasone paid $5,000 for his franchise. Two years later, the team signed its first big star, sharpshooting forward and future Hall-of-Famer Dolph Schayes. Like the Warriors, Syracuse became part of the NBA after the merger of the BAA and NBL. The Nationals immediately made their mark, going 51–13 in the regular season and defeating the Warriors in the first round of the playoffs. But Syracuse lost to the Minneapolis Lakers in the NBA Finals, four games to two.

After more near misses, the Nationals broke through in the 1954-55 season, defeating the Fort Wayne Pistons in seven games for the NBA championship. The Game 7 hero was George King, a lowly eighth-round draft choice in 1950. King drained a free throw with 12 seconds remaining to give Syracuse a 92–91 lead, and then stole the inbounds pass to seal the win. Though the Nationals never won another title, they established a remarkable record of consistency by making the playoffs in each of their 14 seasons. Besides Schayes, other key players during this time were fellow Hall of Fame guard Hal Greer and center John Kerr.

Despite the Nationals' on-court success, by the early 1960s, they were the NBA's only remaining small-market franchise. In that era, ticket sales were almost the only source of revenue for sports teams. Syracuse struggled to fill seats in the league's smallest arena. Biasone—who loved Syracuse and loved his team—had repeatedly denied that the Nationals were for sale. But early in 1963, he finally had to face facts: his team would lose large amounts of money in the upcoming season. Reluctantly, Biasone sold the Nationals.

The transition from Syracuse to Philadelphia was challenging for everyone, including fans in the new city. Even the much-anticipated November matchup between the 76ers and Warriors drew just 5,800 people, and far fewer fans attended most other games. The 76ers' inaugural season ended with a disappointing 34–46 record and a plea from co-owner Ike

INTRODUCING...

HAL GREER

POSITION GUARD / FORWARD
HEIGHT 6-FOOT-2
NATIONALS / 76ERS
SEASONS 1958–73

Hal Greer played for the same franchise his entire 15-year career, from the day he signed with the Syracuse Nationals in 1958 through the team's 1963 reincarnation as the Philadelphia 76ers and a decade after that. He gave the same sterling performance year after year, averaging 19.2 points and finishing his career with 21,586 points. His teammates were both bigger and more boisterous than he was, but Greer quietly earned the respect of his peers, his opponents, and Philadelphia fans. "If there were an award given for a player who is most respected by basketball insiders while getting the minimum public appreciation, Greer could win hands down," wrote a sports reporter for the Philadelphia *Herald Tribune* in the mid-1960s. Greer garnered his fair share of awards, including being named an All-Star 10 times and earning All-Star Game MVP honors in 1968. But what mattered most to the Hall of Fame guard was that fans remembered how hard he played every day. "Consistency," he said. "For me, that was the thing ... I would like to be remembered as a great, consistent player."

15

COURTSIDE STORIES

HITTING THE CENTURY MARK

Hershey, Pennsylvania, is nicknamed the "Sweetest Place on Earth." It certainly was sweet for Wilt Chamberlain on March 2, 1962, as the Warriors took on the New York Knicks there. The league's top scorer, Chamberlain poured in 23 points in the first quarter and added 18 in the second. In the locker room, guard Guy Rodgers said, "Let's get the ball to Dip [short for Chamberlain's nickname "the Big Dipper"]. Let's see how many he can get." It didn't take long to find out. Despite being triple-teamed and frequently fouled, Chamberlain scored 28 points in the third quarter. His pace slowed a little in the fourth, as he netted just six points in the first four minutes. His teammates encouraged him, sometimes passing up open shots of their own to feed him the ball. Their tactics paid off, as Chamberlain made his 100th point of the night with 46 seconds remaining. That game defined him as a player. "I get constant reminders from fans who equate that game and my career as one and the same," Chamberlain said years later. "That's my tag, whether I like it or not."

Richman for more support. "We have a solid core of about 1,000 loyal fans," he says. "Next year, this should increase to about 2,500 for every game."

Richman tried to entice larger crowds by bringing hometown hero Wilt Chamberlain back to Philly in 1965. "The Big Dipper" and Billy "The Kangaroo Kid" Cunningham, an aggressive rookie forward, gave Philadelphia fans plenty to cheer about. Under new coach Alex Hannum, the 76ers finished the 1966–67 season 68–13, the best mark in NBA history at the time.

The mighty 76ers breezed past the Cincinnati Royals and Boston Celtics in the first two rounds of the playoffs, then they fittingly wrapped up the NBA title by trouncing the Warriors

in six games. "I honestly don't know when I've been happier," Hannum said. "This is the greatest team ever assembled." It boasted four future Hall of Famers—Chamberlain, Greer, Cunningham, and forward Chet Walker.

That dominant team returned almost entirely intact for the following season and again won more than 60 games, averaging 122.6 points in each one. Although Philadelphia took a commanding three-games-to-one lead in the Eastern Division finals, the Boston Celtics rallied to push the series to a deciding Game 7. With the 76ers down by two with seconds remaining in the fourth quarter, Greer raced down the court. But Boston's Hall of Fame forward John Havlicek picked off Greer's pass, and the Celtics won.

DR. J CURES THE 76ERS' AILMENTS

BILLY CUNNINGHAM AVERAGED 23.3 POINTS PER GAME DURING THE 1971–72 SEASON.

That disappointing defeat was the tip of the iceberg. During the off-season, Chamberlain was traded, and Coach Hannum resigned. The team pinned its hopes for the future on Cunningham, Greer, and Archie Clark, a fleet-footed guard obtained in the Chamberlain trade.

Although the 76ers returned to the playoffs each of the next three seasons, they were overmatched each time. When a dismal 30–52 record kept Philadelphia out of the playoffs for the first time in team history in 1972, no one thought things could get much worse. But they did. The 76ers began the 1972–73 season with 15 straight losses and ended an unbelievable 9–73, at that time the worst-ever NBA record. Local media mockingly referred to the team as the "9-and-73ers."

A PATRIOTIC NAME

Purchasing an NBA franchise for Philadelphia in 1963 was a difficult—and costly—move for Irv Kosloff, owner of a large paper company, and attorney Ike Richman. However, picking a name to replace the Nationals wasn't. The owners asked for suggestions and received 500 different ideas from more than 4,000 fans. Their favorite came from a man named Walter Stahlberg, whose submission of "76ers" justified the name by saying, "No athletic team has ever paid tribute to the gallant men who forged this country's independence, and certainly, Philadelphia, shrine of liberty, should do so." Kosloff and Richman agreed on those grounds—but they also liked the sound of the name. Richman's son, Mike, remembered the day his dad announced that the decision had been made. The family was driving to a resort in upstate New York for an NBA charity game when he told them. "He just said it was catchy and fast," Mike explained. Stahlberg won a lifetime pass to 76ers games, plus an all-expenses-paid trip to California to see Philadelphia's former team, the San Francisco Warriors, take on the city's new club.

Philadelphia had nowhere to go but up. Guard Fred Carter and forward Tom Van Arsdale paired up to lead the 76ers toward respectability with a 25–57 record in 1973–74 and a 34–48 mark the next season, although neither effort was good enough for the playoffs.

The pace picked up for the 76ers in the summer of 1975, when the team signed brawny forward George McGinnis, named the Most Valuable Player (MVP) of the American Basketball Association (ABA) the previous year. In 1975–76, McGinnis and his reliable jump shot helped the team return to the playoffs after a four-year absence.

hiladelphia's recovery was complete when new owner Fitz Eugene Dixon Jr. spent $6 million to obtain forward Julius "Dr. J" Erving. Erving was an incredible athlete and entertaining performer whose amazing fakes and soaring dunks thrilled fans. His arrival pleased his new teammates as well. "When I heard that Doc was coming, I just fell down to my knees and cried," said Philadelphia center Caldwell Jones. "At least I don't have to worry about him going to the hoop on me."

Erving sparked the surging 76ers to the Eastern Conference crown in 1976–77. He and McGinnis combined to average more than 40 points per game during the regular season and were expected to power through the playoffs as well. Although Philadelphia made the NBA Finals, the Portland Trail Blazers dashed its championship dreams in six games.

Cunningham, who had retired after the 1976 season, returned as coach in 1977. He didn't try to rein in Erving's highflying flair or the enthusiasm of burly center Darryl Dawkins—a colorful character who bestowed names on each of his colossal dunks—but Cunningham did appreciate the unselfish play of forward Bobby Jones and the quiet strength of guard Maurice "Mo" Cheeks, who joined the team in 1978. After having enjoyed a successful run in the previous postseason, the 76ers were disappointingly eliminated by the San Antonio Spurs in the second round of the 1979 playoffs.

Though the 76ers were the underdogs in the next year's playoffs, they upset the Boston Celtics in the conference finals and faced the Los Angeles Lakers in the NBA Finals. Dr. J and Dawkins fought hard against their star counterparts—Lakers guard Magic Johnson and center Kareem Abdul-Jabbar—but the Lakers rode Johnson's 42-point effort to a series-ending win in Game 6. "Magic was outstanding," conceded 76ers guard Doug Collins. "I knew he was good, but I never realized he was great."

JULIUS ERVING

POSITION FORWARD / GUARD
HEIGHT 6-FOOT-6
76ERS SEASONS
1976–87

People noticed Julius Erving's hands first. "Dr. J" wore size 11 gloves—the largest made—and needed a size 13.5 ring when the 76ers won the 1983 NBA championship. Those huge hands helped him control the basketball with an ease that other players admired and envied. He was palming the ball by the time he was in seventh grade, about the same time he started using his powerful legs and long arms to throw dunks through the hoop. "I guess I consider my hands my best physical attribute," he said. "But I don't like to forget my legs either." No one could forget those legs; Erving's highflying dunks thrilled fans. His 1983 "rock the baby" dunk, in which he rocked the ball gently before slinging it behind his head and jumping over Los Angeles Lakers guard Michael Cooper to slam it through the hoop, is considered one of the greatest dunks of all time. But Dr. J's skills went far beyond dunking. He scored 30,026 points in his career in the NBA and ABA, the fifth-highest total in pro hoops history.

PHILADELPHIA FEELING

ALL-STAR MOSES MALONE AND A TALENTED ROSTER AIMED FOR AN NBA CHAMPIONSHIP.

The 76ers looked for a little magic of their own after losing to the Lakers again in the 1982 Finals. Although Dr. J was at the top of his game, and his teammates—including sharpshooting guard Andrew Toney—had on-court chemistry, something seemed to be missing. That "something" turned out to be veteran center Moses Malone. With Malone on board and winning MVP honors, the 76ers creamed the competition in the East, finishing the 1982–83 season with a 65–17 record. As they headed into the playoffs, Malone told reporters that the outcome would be "Fo, fo, fo," predicting that his team would sweep each postseason opponent in four games.

Except for the five-game series against the Milwaukee Bucks in the second round, it turned out exactly as Malone had foreseen. The 76ers waltzed through the postseason and swept the Lakers in the four-game Finals series. Erving

CHAMPIONSHIP CITY

When the Philadelphia 76ers squared off against the Los Angeles Lakers in the 1980 NBA Finals, they started a citywide trend. Over the next nine months, three of the city's other professional sports teams would play for their respective league championships. Only one of those teams, however, would actually win. The 76ers lost in six games to the Lakers. Eight days later, the National Hockey League's Philadelphia Flyers fell to the New York Islanders in Game 6 of the Stanley Cup Finals. And in January 1981, Philadelphia's National Football League franchise, the Eagles, lost Super Bowl XV to the Oakland Raiders. Only Major League Baseball's Philadelphia Phillies saved the city from a four-way championship shutout. The Phillies won their first World Series in October, capturing the title with a Game 6 win over the Kansas City Royals at Veterans Stadium in Philadelphia. "Everybody said we couldn't win," Phillies shortstop Larry Bowa said after the victory. "The Phillies aren't good enough. They don't have the heart, they don't have the character. We have all of the above."

proudly hoisted the NBA championship trophy while Philadelphia fans celebrated. "There was nothing pretty about what we did to the NBA this year," he said. "It was beautiful."

Virtually the same 76ers squad returned the following season but without the same results. Despite tallying 52 wins in 1983–84, the 76ers lost a wild five-game, first-round playoff series against the upstart New Jersey Nets. Philadelphia would founder in the playoffs each of the next two seasons as well.

In 1984, some of the attention shifted from Dr. J to "Sir Charles"—forward Charles Barkley, a fierce competitor built more like a football lineman than a basketball star. His youthful enthusiasm sparked the aging Sixers to a 58–24 record and wins in the first two rounds of the playoffs. But when Philadelphia faced Boston in the conference finals, the 76ers' postseason ended abruptly.

That was the beginning of the end. Injuries sidelined Toney for the entire 1985–86 season and hobbled Malone as the team fell to the Bucks in the second round of the playoffs. Malone was then traded during the off-season, and Erving retired in 1987. In 1988, Philadelphia

was shut out of the playoffs for the first time in 12 seasons.

Barkley had an incredible 1987–88 season, leading the team in scoring with 28.3 points per game and ranking sixth in league-wide rebounding. But even with the help of forward Cliff Robinson, he couldn't stop the 76ers' slide. The next season, the team brought in rookie guard Hersey Hawkins and swingman Ron Anderson, who teamed with Barkley to lead Philadelphia back to a winning record and a spot in the postseason. But the New York Knicks bounced them in the first round.

Still, Philadelphia's prospects seemed to be improving. The team won the Atlantic Division in 1990 before falling to the surging Chicago Bulls in the second round of the playoffs. The 76ers returned to the playoffs again the next year but were stopped short of the conference finals.

Although Barkley remained among the league leaders in scoring and rebounding year in and year out, the forceful forward grew weary of Philadelphia's stumbling in the playoffs. When the 76ers' 1991–92 season ended with a 10th-place conference finish, Barkley demanded to be traded. He was sent to the Phoenix Suns, where he promptly earned MVP honors.

MAURICE CHEEKS

**POSITION GUARD
HEIGHT 6-FOOT-1
76ERS SEASONS
1978-89**

Stars surrounded Maurice Cheeks during his entire 11-year tenure with the Philadelphia 76ers, and his quiet achievements were often overshadowed by the amazing accomplishments of teammates Julius Erving, Moses Malone, and Charles Barkley. But Cheeks's less-glamorous contributions helped the team win—and made him a favorite of Philadelphia's hardworking fans. Those fans appreciated his unselfish play almost as much as they relished how often he stole the ball from opposing players. When Cheeks retired from the NBA in 1993, he was the all-time leader in steals, having averaged more than two per game. "He would always steal at least one ball from me, every game," said Milwaukee Bucks guard Brian Winters. "As long as it was only one, I was happy." Cheeks himself was all about making people happy. He will always be remembered for rushing to the side of a 13-year-old girl singing the national anthem at a game in Portland, where he coached from 2001 to 2005. She had forgotten the words, and he ran out to help her finish. "That's just so Maurice," a friend said later. "That's the essence of him."

IVERSON IS "THE ANSWER"

THE ARRIVAL OF FEISTY POINT GUARD ALLEN IVERSON MARKED A NEW ERA FOR THE TEAM.

Philadelphia did not fare well after Barkley's exit. Although they had picked up versatile guard Jeff Hornacek in the Barkley trade and drafted explosive forward Clarence Weatherspoon, the 76ers won just 26 games in 1992–93. The team would be hard pressed to tally even that many victories during each of the next four seasons.

As the club struggled, Philadelphia kept trying to find the right combination of coaches and players. Before the 1993–94 season, the 76ers released several players, traded Hawkins for point guard Dana Barros, and hired former guard Fred Carter as coach. They used the second pick of the 1993 NBA Draft to bring in 7-foot-6 center Shawn Bradley. When the year ended with a lackluster 25–57 record, Carter was replaced by former Spurs coach John Lucas. There were some bright spots: Bradley was

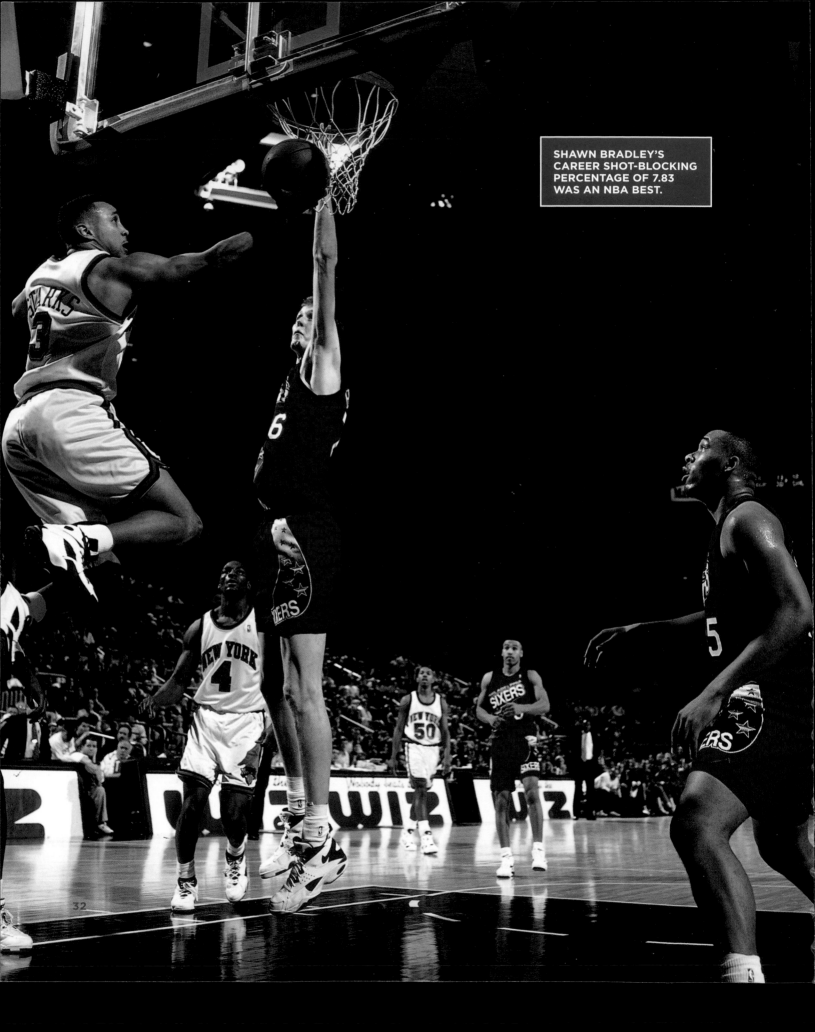

SHAWN BRADLEY'S CAREER SHOT-BLOCKING PERCENTAGE OF 7.83 WAS AN NBA BEST.

becoming a solid shot blocker, and Barros began earning a reputation as one of the league's most dangerous point guards. But injuries slowed the team's overall progress.

The revolving roster wreaked havoc during the 1995–96 season, with more than 20 players rotating on and off the court. Philadelphia finished 18–64; only the expansion Vancouver Grizzlies had a worse record. All those losses gave the 76ers the first pick in the 1996 NBA Draft, with which they selected Georgetown University point guard Allen Iverson. "He's a special athlete and a special competitor, and he has leadership ability," general manager Brad Greenberg said on draft day. "He made it an easy decision."

The 76ers hoped that Iverson would live up to his nickname, "The Answer." As a rookie, Iverson racked up 23.5 points per game, 7.5 assists, and 4.1 rebounds in 1996–97, proving that he could break down opposing defenses better than anyone else in the league. "I try to put pressure on the defense," Iverson explained. "I am always, always looking to score, always looking to make something happen on the court."

Iverson and highflying swingman Jerry Stackhouse became one of the highest-scoring duos in the league, yet Philadelphia improved to only 22–60 in 1996–97. The team's answer was persuading longtime NBA coach Larry Brown to come to Philadelphia in 1997. Brown was recognized as a masterful teacher of the game—and the 76ers' roster was full of young, inexperienced students.

Brown quickly overhauled that roster. By the end of the 1997–98 season, only five players he had started with still remained as he rebuilt the team around Iverson and hustling guard Eric Snow. In the 1998–99 season, the 76ers returned to the playoffs for the first time since 1991. Appreciative Philadelphia fans filled the arena with signs saying, "Allen Iverson for MVP" and "Larry Brown, Coach of the Year." The most prophetic, however, said, "We'll Be Back."

UP AND DOWN ... AND UP AGAIN?

AARON McKIE NEVER GAINED SUPERSTAR STATUS BUT BECAME A SIXERS FAN FAVORITE.

Although a thumb injury sidelined Iverson to begin the next season, the lightning-quick guard led the team in scoring for 22 straight games when he returned. With help from veteran forward Toni Kukoc, who recorded the team's first triple-double—19 points, 10 rebounds, and 10 assists—in 5 years, Iverson took the team back to the playoffs in 2000. The Indiana Pacers handed another loss to the 76ers in a six-game, second-round series. But the team and its fans could see the potential building in this exuberant young club. Attendance records had been shattered, and fans were confident that their patience was about to pay off.

They were right. In 2000–01, the 76ers opened with a decisive 101–72 victory over the Knicks, and then went on to win their next nine games as well. Injuries slowed Snow and Iverson, but backup shooting guard Aaron McKie

CHARLES BARKLEY

POSITION FORWARD
HEIGHT 6-FOOT-6
76ERS SEASONS
1984–92

When Charles Barkley entered the NBA in 1984, he was saddled with an unfortunate nickname: "The Round Mound of Rebound," a reference to his portly stature and skill at grabbing boards. By the end of his rookie season, however, he was called "Sir Charles," in deference to his ruling over the court. "He plays everything," said former center Bill Walton. "There is nobody who does what Barkley does. He's a dominant rebounder, a dominant defensive player, a three-point shooter, a dribbler, a playmaker." Barkley's greatness as a player was rivaled only by his outrageous behavior and outspoken nature off the court. His controversial comments and impulsive actions (including once spitting at a heckling fan in New Jersey, only to have his spittle land on a little girl) often made headlines in the media. Barkley's behavior irritated 76ers ownership almost as much as the team's string of losing seasons bothered Barkley. When he asked for a trade in 1992, the 76ers sent the future Hall-of-Famer to Phoenix. Fans booed when he returned to play against Philadelphia the following season.

SIX-FOOT-11 CENTER SAMUEL DALEMBERT MISSED ONE OF NINE SIXERS SEASONS BECAUSE OF INJURY.

stepped up and recorded back-to-back triple-doubles in the process. He was named the NBA's Sixth Man of the Year. More importantly, however, his team won its division and then took three playoff series to surge to the NBA Finals.

The 76ers faced the heavily favored Lakers in the Finals but pulled off a stunning upset in Game 1. Iverson scored 48 points and quickly quieted L.A. fans who shouted "Sweep!" as the game began. "I'm glad nobody bet their life on [a sweep], because they'd be dead by now," Iverson said. "Everyone said we can't do it, and that drives us." That drive, however, was overridden by the sheer talent of the Lakers,

who won the next four games and the title.

Philadelphia lost its first five games the next season en route to a mediocre 43–39 record. Although the 76ers returned to the playoffs after each of the next two seasons, they lost in early rounds both times. Larry Brown abruptly left Philadelphia in May 2003 to become head coach of the Detroit Pistons. In the transitional season that followed, Philadelphia struggled for wins and finished out of playoff contention.

Sixers management tweaked the roster again, selecting talented young forward Andre Iguodala in the 2004 Draft and bringing in veteran forward Chris Webber. But early in

COURTSIDE STORIES

LISTENING TO THE ZINK

From the 1940s through the 1980s, Philadelphia sports fans knew that no matter how their home team performed on any given day, they would still be entertained. That's because public address announcer Dave "The Zink" Zinkoff—who worked at Philadelphia Phillies, Warriors, and 76ers games—always delivered a fabulous performance. In his bold, nasally voice, he told fans that smoking was not permitted, but if anyone decided to light up, "please do not exhale." Zinkoff was best known for his animated introduction of 76ers star forward Julius Erving: "Number 6, Julius, the Doctor, Errrrrrrrrving!" Fans also loved his classic call as the game wound down: "Twooo minutes left in this ballgame." The Zink's announcements were so memorable that even opposing players delighted in trying to imitate them. Zinkoff, whose career highlights included calling center Wilt Chamberlain's historic 100-point game with the Warriors in 1962, was also known for presenting congratulatory salamis to players after particularly good performances. The Zink died on Christmas Day, 1985; on March 25, 1986, his microphone was retired by the 76ers.

FORWARD ELTON BRAND AVERAGED 13.8 POINTS A GAME DURING HIS FIRST PHILLY SEASON.

2006–07, Iverson called a meeting with team management and issued an ultimatum: find players to help me win or trade me. Two weeks later, in mid-December, he was sent to the Denver Nuggets for guard Andre Miller and forward Joe Smith. Soon after, the aging Webber was released.

The continuous upheaval took a heavy toll as Philadelphia missed the postseason two years in a row. When the team finally made it back in 2008, it was eliminated by the Pistons in the first round. Before the next season, Philadelphia signed forward Elton Brand and brought in guards Royal Ivey and Louis Williams, placing the future success of the team in their hands. Iguodala ranked among the league leaders in steals and assists during the 2008–09 season,

helping carry the 76ers back to the playoffs and becoming a fan favorite along the way. Iguodala could not take all the credit, though. "It's that Philadelphia style of play," he said. "Everybody is a hard worker. I think as a team we bring that to the table."

espite the addition of top draft choice point guard Jrue Holiday and the return of Allen Iverson, Philadelphia struggled to a 27–55 mark in 2009–10. Iverson left before the end of the season, and the team felt restricted by the offensive system that new coach Eddie Jordan implemented. He was fired at the end of the season, with former 76ers

ENERGETIC FORWARD THADDEUS YOUNG WAS DRAFTED IN 2007 AS THE 12TH OVERALL PICK.

SWINGMAN EVAN TURNER'S PER-GAME ASSISTS AVERAGE IMPROVED AFTER HIS ROOKIE SEASON.

ALLEN IVERSON

In professional basketball, Allen Iverson was considered small. But what the 165-pound guard lacked in size, he more than made up for in hustle and attitude. He was so impressive during his first two seasons at Georgetown University that Philadelphia drafted him with the first overall pick in the 1996 NBA Draft. Although his heavily tattooed body caught some fans off guard, his confident play and aggressive gamesmanship were welcome catalysts for the slumping team. He was named Rookie of the Year for 1996–97, and four years later, took home the league's MVP trophy and led his team to the NBA Finals. In the process of attaining such honors, Iverson also gained recognition as one of the most prolific scorers in the game—which didn't surprise the young guard at all. "I believe in my heart I'm the best player in the world," he said after scoring 58 points in a 2002 game. "I'm just a scorer." He scored 21,292 points for the 76ers before being traded partway through the 2006–07 season. In 2009, he returned for part of a final season.

ANDRE IGUODALA

COURTSIDE STORIES
ADDING BY SUBTRACTING

After the 2011–12 season, many NBA experts felt the 76ers didn't have a dominant center nor a proven big-time scoring threat. A solution to those problems began to emerge when the Orlando Magic's All-Star center Dwight Howard demanded a trade. At first, the 76ers tried to make a straight swap. When that didn't work out, they involved the Denver Nuggets and Los Angeles Lakers. Several weeks and countless phone calls later, the teams worked out a complicated four-way deal. Most of the headlines went to Howard's becoming a Laker, but the 76ers added high-scoring swingman Jason Richardson and center Andrew Bynum. "We've gotten bigger, we've gotten stronger, and we've gotten more athletic than we were at this time last year," said 76ers president Rod Thorn. "Andrew is the best center in the East." The cost was high, as Philadelphia gave up forward Andre Iguodala and three first-round draft choices to pull it off. There was one consolation. The deal wasn't finalized until after the 2012 Summer Olympics, during which Iguodala received a gold medal as a member of the U.S. men's basketball team. He therefore joined Charles Barkley as the only gold-medal-winning 76ers players in franchise history.

"IT'S THAT PHILADELPHIA STYLE OF PLAY. EVERYBODY IS A HARD WORKER. I THINK AS A TEAM WE BRING THAT TO THE TABLE."

— ANDRE IGUODALA ON SIXERS STYLE

guard Doug Collins replacing him.

Philadelphia returned to respectability in the following season, notching a 41–41 mark before being eliminated in the first round of the playoffs. The second overall draft pick, swingman Evan Turner showed considerable promise in his rookie season.

The 76ers opened the lockout-shortened 2011–12 season with a sizzling 20–9 mark but trailed off to finish 35–31 and earn the eighth and final playoff seed in the Eastern Division. They made history by knocking off the injury-riddled Bulls in six games, just the fifth time in NBA history that an eighth seed had defeated a top seed. The season ended with the Celtics defeating Philadelphia four games to three in the next round.

The 76ers sought to bulk up in the paint and add scoring punch by acquiring 7-foot center Andrew Bynum in a four-team trade before the 2012–13 season. Unfortunately, Bynum never played a single game, thanks to knee problems. Though Holiday averaged nearly 18 points a game and 5 other players had double-digit averages, the 76ers tied for last in scoring and

finished 34–48. Still, a swing of just four games would have put them in the playoffs again.

Unfortunately for the 76ers, the 2013–14 campaign took a turn for the worse. Holiday had been traded before the season began, and by February, several key players such as Turner and Bynum were gone as well. Led by new coach Brett Brown, the talents of rookie guard Michael Carter-Williams and forward Thaddeus Young were overshadowed as the 76ers lost 26 games in a row—tying an infamous NBA record. The positive news that came out of such an abysmal season was that the team would have the chance for a top choice in the 2014 Draft. "The ball might not be going in the basket for the Sixers," wrote Zachary Arthur of BleacherReport.com, "but it will soon be in their court."

For all the recent negativity, the fact remains that the Philadelphia 76ers have compiled one of the most prestigious pedigrees in the NBA, making the playoffs 47 times in their 64-year history. Even more impressive, they have played in the Finals nine times—third only to the Celtics and the Lakers—and have claimed the title three times. Philadelphia fans look forward to their team improving for a chance at the NBA title once again.

HIGH-SCORING MICHAEL
CARTER-WILLIAMS HAD
BEEN A STANDOUT AT
SYRACUSE UNIVERSITY.

INDEX

All-Star Game 15

Anderson, Ron 28

Barkley, Charles 28, 29, 31, 37, 44

Barros, Dana 31, 33

Basketball Hall of Fame 14, 15, 17, 37

Biasone, Danny 11, 14

Bradley, Shawn 31

Brand, Elton 41

Brown, Brett 45

Brown, Larry 31, 38

Bynum, Andrew 44, 45

Carter, Fred 21, 31

Carter-Williams, Michael 45

Chamberlain, Wilt 10, 14, 16, 17, 19, 39

Cheeks, Maurice "Mo" 21, 29

Clark, Archie 19

Collins, Doug 21, 45

Cunningham, Billy 17, 19, 21

Dawkins, Darryl 21

division championships 28, 38

Dixon, Fitz Eugene 21

Eastern Conference finals 21

Eastern Division finals 17

Erving, Julius 21, 23, 25, 28, 29, 39

Greenberg, Brad 33

Greer, Hal 14, 15, 17, 19

Hannum, Alex 10, 17, 19

Hawkins, Hersey 28, 31

Holiday, Jrue 41, 45

Hornacek, Jeff 31

Iguodala, Andre 38, 41, 44

Iverson, Allen 33, 35, 38, 41, 43

Ivey, Royal 41

Jones, Bobby 21

Jones, Caldwell 21

Jordan, Eddie 41

Kerr, John 14

King, George 14

Kosloff, Irv 20

Kukoc, Toni 35

Lucas, John 31

Malone, Moses 25, 28, 29

McGinnis, George 21

McKie, Aaron 35, 38

Miller, Andre 41

MVP award 25, 43

NBA championships 14, 17, 23, 25, 28, 45

NBA Finals 14, 21, 25, 27, 38, 43, 45

NBA records 17, 19, 45

Olympics 44

Philadelphia Warriors 10, 14, 16, 39

playoffs 14, 17, 19, 21, 25, 28, 33, 35, 38, 41, 45

Richardson, Jason 44

Richman, Isaac "Ike" 14, 17, 20

Robinson, Cliff 28

Rookie of the Year award 43

Schayes, Dolph 12, 14

Sixth Man of the Year award 38

Smith, Joe 41

Snow, Eric 33, 35

Stackhouse, Jerry 33

Stahlberg, Walter 20

Syracuse Nationals 11, 12, 14, 15

relocation to Philadelphia 12, 14, 15

team name 20

team records 14, 17, 19, 21, 28, 31, 33, 38, 41, 45

Thorn, Rod 44

Toney, Andrew 25, 28

Turner, Evan 45

Van Arsdale, Tom 21

Walker, Chet 17

Weatherspoon, Clarence 31

Webber, Chris 38, 41

Williams, Louis 41

Young, Thaddeus 45

Zinkoff, Dave 39

WITHDRAWN